ISLAM

Alan Brine

General Inspector, RE, for Hampshire

SERIES EDITOR: CLIVE ERRICKER
Lecturer in Arts Education
University of Warwick

Longman

About the Themes in Religion series

This series of books offers a lively and accessible introduction to the six main world religions for students taking GCSE Religious Studies. The books can be used separately to study one religious tradition, or they can be used together, to investigate one theme across the traditions, such as beliefs, worship, pilgrimage or values. The section on values shows how each religion reacts to everyday life and the modern world. The spreads offer class activities and assignments that relate to coursework requirements and encourage further research, and each book provides a glossary of important terms and a reading list.

Each spread is self-contained and presents an important aspect of each religion. Through carefully chosen photographs, clear text and relevant quotations from scriptures and believers, students will learn about each religion and the living impact it has for believers today. The wide variety of assignments help pupils to evaluate what they have read, suggest activities to further their understanding, and raise issues for them to reflect on.

We hope that these books will provide students of all abilities with a stimulating introduction to these religions, and that the enjoyment of using them matches that of producing them.

Clive Erricker

022269
297

About Islam

Developing an appreciation of the distinctive character of the Islamic tradition is a primary need in the contemporary world. This book addresses that need by focusing on the cultural ideas and experiences that characterise the Muslim way of life. The text and photographs convey the diversity of the tradition and allow the student to engage in a positive way with the issues that are central to the Muslim vision.

The opening sections on belief and scriptures provide a framework within which the significance of worship, celebrations, pilgrimage and the values of Islam can be understood. Students are encouraged to develop their understanding by focusing on specific examples of the ways in which Muslims express their experiences – in poetry, art, movement and dance, as well as through personal statements about the meaning of their faith.

Alan Brine

Thank You
I would like to thank Muhammad Riyami for his invaluable help in writing this book.

For Lucy and Becky

CONTENTS

BELIEFS

WHAT REALLY MATTERS?

In this book we will explore the things which Muslims value and think are important. We will be hearing from Muslims about their own views and trying to understand the answers they give. Before we begin, however, we need to recognise that we probably have some mental pictures about Muslims and Islam already. The picture shows a Muslim on the annual pilgrimage to Makkah. We will be finding out about this later in the book. For the moment, look carefully at the picture before doing the activity that follows.

⬤ With a partner, write down a list of five or six things which you think of when you hear the words Muslim or Islam. As a class, group your ideas together. How many of the ideas give a good impression of the religion and how many give a bad impression? Where do you think you got the ideas from? Discuss which of the ideas you think Muslims might highlight as being important to them.

What really matters to a Muslim?

⬤ As human beings we all have some kind of idea about what really matters to us in life. How would you explain what matters to you? Find some way of representing this in the form of a symbol or image.

We asked one Muslim to tell us how she would answer the question:

'For me, as a Muslim, what really matters can be summed up in one short sentence:

There is no God but Allah and Muhammad is His Prophet.

We call this sentence our Declaration of Faith or, in Arabic, the Shahadah. It may seem a simple thing but it will take me all my life to understand it. Even then I will never fully grasp the mystery of these simple words.'

This Muslim Declaration of Faith, the **Shahadah**, is the first of the five **Pillars of Islam** which are the heart of the religion. One way of describing Muslims is to say that they are people who decide to follow the five Pillars of Islam in their daily life.

ASSIGNMENTS

⬤ Carry out a survey of people to find out what mental pictures they have of Islam. Write a short commentary on your findings. Are some images of Islam more common than others? How far do you think the pictures are based on good information or on prejudice and stereotypes?

⬤ The five Pillars of Islam were mentioned above. Find out what they are and write a short description of each.

⬤ In the quote above, the Muslim woman said that what really mattered to her was a mystery and it would take her the rest of her life to understand it. Write a piece to explain what you think she meant.

KEY WORDS

Shahadah   Pillars of Islam

THERE IS NO GOD BUT ALLAH

● The picture shows one way in which Muslims represent their understanding of God. Discuss how this is different from ways in which other religions portray God.

The word **Allah** is simply the Arabic name for God. Muslims throughout the world, even if they do not normally speak Arabic, use the word 'Allah' to speak of God. Muslims never represent God with any form of picture. They believe it is quite wrong to create any image of God. One Muslim explained:

'The Qur'an, our sacred book, tells us: "Like to Allah there is nothing." In other words, God is beyond anything I can understand. There is nothing like God, so nothing looks like God. How then could I picture God? Other religions try to picture what God is like, but the danger of this is that you end up worshipping the picture and not God.'

The Beautiful Names of God

Instead of trying to create pictures of God, Muslims believe there are 99 names which help them understand Allah. The picture shows these 99 names arranged in a pattern. The names are described as Beautiful, and Muslims will often repeat the names and reflect on their meaning. They also create works of art to show these Beautiful Names in an elegant and attractive way. Among the names are: The One, The Hearer, The Light, The All-Aware, The Inward, The Merciful, The Guide, The Creator, The Sustainer, The Truth.

● Discuss any similarities or differences between these words and the words which other religions use to speak of God.

Tawhid

Of all the Beautiful Names of God, one is perhaps the most helpful in understanding Allah. That is – The One. The name is a clue to a central Muslim belief: **Tawhid**.

'Tawhid is the most important Islamic belief. It implies that everything on this earth originates from the one and only Creator who is also the Sustainer and the sole Source of Guidance. The Creator and Source of Guidance is one and the same and therefore deserves worship and obedience from mankind. There is no scope for any partnership. Tawhid is pure monotheism. It tells man that Allah is neither born nor is anyone born of Him. He has no son or daughter. He is Allah, the One.'

ASSIGNMENTS

● Imagine you are a Muslim parent and you decide to write to your local school to explain why it would be wrong to ask your child to draw a picture of God. Write the letter setting out your reasons.

● How do you understand the link between the idea of Tawhid and the refusal of Muslims to create any pictures of Allah? Write a piece explaining why you think it might be a helpful or dangerous thing to create pictures or images of God.

● It was mentioned above that Muslims often reflect on the Beautiful Names of God. Take one of the names that are used and discuss with a partner what you think the value of reflecting on this name might be.

KEY WORDS

Allah   Tawhid

ISLAM: PEACE AND SUBMISSION

People often use the word **Islam** as a name for a religion which began 1,400 years ago. While it is true that the Holy Prophet Muhammad lived about 1,400 years ago, Muslims are unhappy about the idea that their religion was started by Muhammad. For Muslims, Islam has existed since the time of creation. Muhammad was the Last Prophet who brought the final revelation. He was not the founder of the religion of Islam.

To understand this we need to know what the word 'Islam' means. The word has two basic meanings in Arabic: peace and submission. So someone who follows the religion of Islam, in other words a Muslim, is someone who is seeking to become peaceful and submissive.

Peace and submission

● Make two lists of any words you link with 'peace' and 'submission'. How many words are common to both lists? Probably not very many. Can you make any sense of the idea that there is a link between the words 'peace' and 'submission'?

● Look at the picture. It is a garden in the Muslim palace of the Alhambra in Granada, Spain. The scene is very peaceful, but does it also make any sense to say it is a picture of submission?

It is very important to understand the meaning of the word 'Islam'. Muslims place great importance on the idea that God is One and has no partner. They understand that we will only find peace when we realise that nothing which happens on earth is independent of God. So we are totally dependent on Allah. If we forget this and imagine we can live independent lives, we will lose our sense of peace. True peacefulness will only come when we realise that we, and everything else, are dependent on God alone.

A Muslim viewpoint

'Being submissive is not about being weak or living like a robot. It is simply understanding that Allah is the Creator of everything. As I come to understand that I am God's creature and that God has breathed something of His spirit into me, then I find I become more peaceful and at ease about my life on earth. This feeling influences the way I see other things around me. All created things are at peace if they carry out the way of life for which they were created. The planets, plants and animals carry out their purpose naturally. They are truly Muslim. They naturally submit to God's purpose and are at peace.'

ASSIGNMENTS

● Think back to your ideas about 'peace' and 'submission'. Discuss whether your ideas have now altered. Do you understand the Muslim viewpoint more clearly? Look again at the picture. Imagine you have been asked to give a brief talk to explain how the palace garden is a good example of the meaning of the word 'Islam'. Write the talk.

● Imagine you are a young Muslim living in Britain. You know that many of the newspaper stories and pictures about Islam show scenes of violence and conflict. You decide to create your own collage of pictures to explain that the meaning of Islam is to do with peacefulness and submission to God. Create the collage and write a short piece to explain what you are trying to say with your pictures.

KEY WORDS

Islam

SHIRK: FORGETTING GOD

Conflicts often seem to be part of everyday life. Violence and suffering occur in many different ways.

The media is full of images like the one below reflecting the many ways in which conflict occurs

● Give some examples of the variety of ways in which:
  a) human beings are in conflict with each other
  b) human beings feel conflict within themselves
  c) human beings are in conflict with the natural world.
Once you have listed the various kinds of conflict, discuss why you think these conflicts occur. What creates conflict?

A Muslim view of conflict and suffering

Recall the idea we explored in the first pages of the book when we talked about what 'really matters' to a Muslim. Reread the statement called the Shahadah. For Muslims, the source of all suffering and conflict is that human beings have a tendency to forget that 'There is no God but Allah.'

The Muslim word to explain the cause of human suffering is **Shirk**. The word means giving God a partner. A Muslim explained the Islamic picture of human life:

'Our life is complicated by many different pressures and distractions. We have many different desires and interests which compete with one another for our attention.
Our activities and thoughts will not be in harmony unless we find the true centre of life.

As human beings we have a tendency to forget what lies at the heart of life. Our experience is complicated. We forget that all creation stems from God. All creation depends on God for its existence and its meaning. Creation has one centre – Allah.

There can only be one centre to life. If you try to live with two centres or choose the wrong centre for your life then you will never find peace and harmony.

Therefore Allah can have no partner. If you think there is any other centre to life apart from Allah you will find your life loses its harmony and peace.'

Muslims believe that, left to themselves, plants and animals are in harmony and balance with each other. They naturally live out their lives in the way they were created to do. The greatness and tragedy of human beings is that we have the freedom to choose how we live our lives. Our problem is that we continually forget that we were created to serve the purpose of Allah. As soon as we forget that, we lose our sense of direction. We then lose our harmony and peace. We lose the centre of our lives. This is the effect of Shirk – creating a partner for Allah.

ASSIGNMENTS

● Take one example from your list of conflicts. Give some thought to how the ideas quoted above might help you to understand that conflict. Share your ideas with a partner.

● Many people experience the loss of a sense of purpose in their lives. They sense that life has no centre. Write a short piece of prose or poetry expressing what these feelings might be like.

● How do you understand the idea that human freedom can be both a greatness and a tragedy? Can you think of any examples which would illustrate this idea?

KEY WORDS

Shirk

REMEMBERING ALLAH

The following poem is from a book of Islamic rhymes for Muslim children:

Allah is Reality
Reality is Light
A compelling goal
The goal is Light.
Light is Allah
Light is Reality
Reality is Allah
Allah is Reality
Allah!
Allah is Reality
Reality is Unity
A compelling goal
The goal is Unity.
Allah is Unity
Unity is Allah
One is Unity
Unity is Allah
Allah is One
Allah! Allah! Allah!

The purpose of the poem is to help children remember that God is the centre of all life. All human problems stem from forgetting that God is this centre; the solution to human problems comes from remembering.

● Read the poem aloud. How many of the ideas you have so far understood about Islam can you find in the poem? What do you notice about the rhythm of the poem? How do you think the ideas and the rhythm might help Muslim children understand their faith?

A history of revelation

Muslims believe that human beings have never been left without a reminder that God is the true centre of life. Throughout history, they say, God has sent revelations to help us to live our lives according to our true purpose. These revelations have come to earth through a series of prophets. Among these prophets were Adam, Abraham, Moses and Jesus. The **Qur'an** is the last of these revelations and was received by the final prophet, Muhammad. A verse from the Qur'an speaks about these prophets:

Say, 'We believe in God, and the revelation given to us and to Abraham, Ishmael, Jacob, and the Tribes, and that given to Moses and Jesus, and that given to all Prophets from their Lord: We make no difference between one and another of them: And we bow to God in Islam.'

A pattern for life

The Qur'an lays out a pattern which will enable Muslims to live their lives in a way which will produce peace and harmony. It is the guidance for their life.

Being a Muslim is not simply a matter of remembering a few ideas. It is a matter of living all your life in ways that enable you to place Allah at the centre of everything you do. Not only prayer, worship and pilgrimage, but every part of life – eating, business, family – should be part of this pattern. The picture shows a Muslim using a string of 99 beads to help him to bring God to his mind.

● From what you know already, what do you think the 99 beads represent?

A North African Muslim using his prayer beads

ASSIGNMENTS

● Look back at the poem at the beginning of this spread. Produce your own poem which could be used to remind yourself of what is important in your own life. Try to create a rhythm in your poem to express your feelings.

● The last five spreads have explained some of the most important Muslim beliefs. Look back over the five pictures which have been used. Write a commentary on each picture explaining how they illustrate some of these key beliefs.

KEY WORDS

Qur'an

THE RECITATION OF ALLAH

RECITE! According to Muslim tradition, this was the first word spoken by God to the Prophet Muhammad. Muhammad did not, according to Muslim belief, write the Qur'an. He simply repeated the message from Allah. This is how one modern Muslim writer expresses Muhammad's experience:

> In the presence of the Revealer Spirit the Prophet's inspired face was illumined, like a mirror; there was silence: conversation stopped as in moments of absence of mind; his body relaxed as if in sleep and a mysterious buzz was heard all around him – as in a telephone conversation where the one who is listening is the only one who can hear distinctly enough to understand.
>
> (Cragg and Speight, *Islam From Within*, Wadsworth)

The illiterate prophet

The word 'recite' is important. By tradition, Muhammad was illiterate. To be asked to 'recite' was asking him to do the impossible. Nevertheless he found he did have the ability to receive the Qur'an. The idea that the Prophet was illiterate may seem surprising. A Muslim explained:

> 'It may appear strange that, as Muslims, we believe the Prophet was unable to read or write. Yet this is very important to us. Because Muhammad was illiterate it means he had never read from the Jewish or Christian scriptures. His mind was not influenced by any other ideas. He was pure when he came to hear the revelations from Allah. It is as if he was a perfect vessel, without any impurities, and so he did not change or taint the message which he received.'

Muslim tradition says that Muhammad received the revelations over the next 22 years. The final revelation came to the Prophet just before his death in 622 CE. He was on his Farewell Pilgrimage to Makkah when he received these words:

> This day have I perfected for you your religion and made My Blessing to you complete, and have chosen Islam as a religion for you.

For Muslims, the meaning of these final words is clear. Allah has given to humanity His final, complete revelation. All the previous revelations to the Prophets before Muhammad have been perfected in the Qur'an. The Prophet Muhammad is the Final Prophet.

ASSIGNMENTS

● The picture shows the cave on Mount Hira, just outside Makkah, where the Prophet Muhammad received the first revelation of the Qur'an. Research some further information about the cave. Either write a piece to explain how he came to visit this cave, or write a poem or piece of prose to express how you think Muhammad felt on this occasion.

● Research and produce a short time-chart showing the key events in the life of the Prophet Muhammad.

● The two longer quotes on this spread express some important ideas. Discuss as a group your reaction to the ideas. Summarise the different thoughts in your group about these accounts of the religious experience of Muhammad.

The cave on Mount Hira, outside Makkah

THE LIGHT OF ISLAM

This mosque lamp is now kept in a museum in London – inside a glass case. It would normally hang near to the place in the mosque where the Qur'an is kept and would contain a small oilwick light.

Like most forms of Muslim art, the lamp is not simply useful and decorative. The design of the object has meaning. This reflects the idea that Islam influences every aspect of Muslim life.

● Before you read any further, study the picture carefully. Note down anything you notice about the shape, decoration, colour or general appearance of the lamp, which you think might be important.

Here is some information which is important in understanding the meaning of the lamp:

The decoration on the lamp includes a quotation from the Qur'an.
The glass of the lamp is not transparent, so you cannot see the light directly. All you see is the glow of the light on the glass. The calligraphy only shows up clearly when the wick is alight.
The shape of the lamp suggests the shape of the human heart.

● 'Have you now got any further ideas about the meaning which the lamp might have for Muslims? Discuss them.

One of the important things about the lamp is that, for Muslims, it shows the importance which the Qur'an has for them. Read the following two passages. The first is from the Qur'an itself; the second explains what the Qur'an means to Muslims.

The likeness of God's light is like a niche
Wherein is a lamp.
The lamp is in a glass, and the glass is, as it were,
A star of brilliance.
The lamp is kindled from a blessed tree.
Light upon Light
God guides to His light whom He will.

'The Qur'an is the guidance for the whole of a Muslim's life. God is completely beyond understanding. The only way to discover God is through His revelation, the Qur'an. God's guidance shines through the Qur'an. If you understand the Qur'an you will come closer to Allah. Allah's light guides through the Qur'an.'

ASSIGNMENTS

● Work with one or two others and try to decide how these passages help you understand the meaning of the lamp. Write a short entry for a guidebook to help a visitor to the museum appreciate what the lamp can tell us about the importance of the Qur'an in the life of a Muslim.

● Create your own design for a mosque lamp. Decide how the shape, colour and decoration might show some of the important ideas about Islam which you have now understood.

THE SIGNIFICANCE OF THE QUR'AN

The goal of devout Muslims is to allow the Qur'an to enter them so completely that their whole lives are shaped by the Word of God. It is not just a matter of learning a set of rules from the Qur'an. The Qur'an has the power to change a person's life.

'I recite from the Qur'an each night before I go to bed. The act of reciting brings a sense of completeness. I feel a unity of my physical and spiritual body and a sense of being united with my Creator. The Qur'an has the power to transform me. I will often recite the Qur'an from memory as I walk. It is remarkable how it creates peace and harmony within you.'

A Chinese Muslim reading his Qur'an

● The picture shows a Muslim with the Qur'an. From what you know already, how would you explain what the difference might be between his experience and the usual experience of reading a book?

The importance and meaning of the Qur'an are expressed in many ways:

When a Qur'an is written, great care is taken with the calligraphy (beautiful handwriting) that is used. The art of producing a Qur'an is a religious act.

In a Muslim home the Qur'an will be carefully wrapped in cloth and placed above any other book in the room.

Verses from the Qur'an are a popular form of Muslim decoration. The Qur'an is present to the eyes of Muslims much of the time.

Children will be taught the Qur'an from an early age.

An ambition of many Muslims is to learn the Qur'an by heart. The name **hafiz** is given to someone who has achieved this. Being a hafiz is valued because it means the Qur'an is present in your mind at all times of day and night.

The Qur'an will be read regularly in the mosque and used on all special occasions: birth, marriage, funerals.

Muslims do not just read the Qur'an. They recite it. It is important that the words are spoken with great care – recognising that the language is poetry rather than prose.

The Qur'an as a bride

Many Muslim poets have tried to describe the value of the Qur'an in their poetry. One of the most famous, Rumi, compared the Qur'an to a bride:

For the Qur'an is a bride who does not show her face to you, even if you draw aside her veil. Should you examine it and not attain happiness or unveiling, it is due to the fact that drawing aside the veil has tricked you. The bride has shown herself as ugly, as if to say: 'I am not that beauty.' But if you do not draw aside the veil and seek only its good pleasure, watering its sown field and attending on it from afar, it will show its face to you.

ASSIGNMENTS

● Try to reproduce a very simple piece of Arabic calligraphy – maybe just a single word. The important thing is to take great care with the task. Try to relax your mind beforehand and produce the calligraphy with gentle free-flowing lines. Remember that Arabic is written from right to left. Discuss with others and write a commentary on the experience afterwards.

● Explain what you understood of the passage from Rumi. How is the Qur'an being compared to a veiled bride?

KEY WORDS

hafiz

THE 'FEEL' OF THE QUR'AN

● The picture shows a page from a copy of the Qur'an. In what ways does the appearance of this book show the importance which Muslims attach to it?

It is difficult to convey the 'feel' of the Qur'an. This quote explains why:

'You can only really get a feel for the Qur'an by listening to it. As Muslims we find that even if we do not fully understand the ideas or the symbols in the Qur'an, we get a real sense of its power when we hear it being recited. That is why we never translate the Qur'an. If you change the language you lose the power and the beauty of the sounds. You sometimes find copies of the Qur'an in English. These are not translations but interpretations of the Qur'an.'

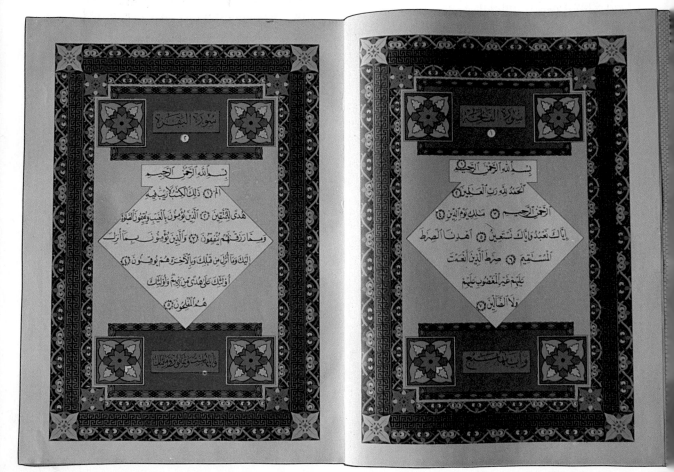

● Discuss how you understand these ideas. If you have someone in the group who is fluent in another language, they may have some ideas about why it is so difficult to translate the 'feel' of words from one language to another. What is the difference between a translation and an interpretation?

Listening to the Qur'an

One Muslim described the effect of listening to the Qur'an being recited:

> As he chanted it was like a man in the wilderness chanting his faith. The voice rose and swelled, changed in tone, became tragic, soared and then floated down on our heads like a seagull gliding gently and softly, little more than a whisper. Peace and everlasting truth were in him and in his voice, while all was crumbling around him.
>
> (*Islam From Within*)

It is common for Muslims to move their bodies very gently while they recite from the Qur'an. The rhythm of the words passes into the whole body. The reciting is a complete experience which affects body, mind and spirit.

Muslims believe that the Qur'an is a unique book. The language is so perfect that it is impossible to believe that it was created by a human hand. The Qur'an itself offers a challenge to anyone who suggests it is not from God:

> 'Do they say he forged it?' Then say: 'Produce a surah like it.'

A **surah** is a chapter in the Qur'an. The challenge is to anyone who doubts that the Qur'an is the Word of God. Muslims believe it is impossible to produce language which has the same quality as the Qur'an itself.

ASSIGNMENTS

● Examine a copy of the Qur'an in English (remembering what was said about translations). Look, in particular, at the surahs towards the end of the Qur'an (e.g. 96, 97, 100– 13). Write a piece summarising your impressions of the book. How is it organised? How would you describe the style of the writing? Do any particular ideas keep reappearing?

● If possible, listen to a section of the Qur'an being read. What impression does the sound make on you?

● Look back to the quote about listening to the Qur'an being recited. How would you explain the writer's experience? What do you think is meant by the two phrases 'all was crumbling around him' and 'like a man in the wilderness'?

● Imagine you are a Muslim who has just overheard someone suggest that the Qur'an is 'just a book'. Look back over the ideas in this section on 'Scriptures' and write a dialogue in which you explain why the Qur'an is more than 'just a book'.

KEY WORDS

surah

THE TRADITIONS OF THE PROPHET

The Apostle of God said: 'Comparing myself to the Prophets who were before me, it is like a man who built a building of great beauty and perfection except for one brick which was missing from one of its corners. People came to walk around it and admire it. They said: "We have never seen such a beautiful building as this, except for that space where the brick is missing." I am that brick.'

These words of the Prophet Muhammad can be found in a collection of traditional stories known as the **Hadith**. This particular story also explains why the Hadith are important.

Muslims do not believe that the Prophet Muhammad was divine. A story about the funeral of the Prophet explains this:

As the Prophet was being buried, one of the leaders of the Muslim community, Abu Bakr, said the following words: 'Anyone who believes that Muhammad still lives, know that he is dead. Anyone who believes that Allah lives, know that Allah lives indeed.'

● What do you understand to be the point of this story?

The perfect human

Although the Prophet is not God, and therefore should not be worshipped, Muslims do believe that Muhammad was the ideal human being. He was perfect. He lived out his whole life in harmony with God. He was not only a spiritual figure, but also a statesman and great political leader of the Muslim community. For this reason, stories about the Prophet's life and teachings are believed to be crucial ways of learning how to live as a perfect Muslim. A great effort is made to ensure that the stories which make up the Hadith are accurate. The following is an example of a story from the Hadith:

The Prophet of God passed by a pile of grain. He put his hand into the middle of it and his fingers found moisture. He exclaimed, 'Merchant, what is this?' The owner of the grain said, 'It has been damaged by the rain, O Prophet of God.' The Prophet replied, 'If that is the case, why not put the damaged grain on top of the pile so that people can see it? Whoever practises fraud is not one of us.'

A Turkish miniature of Muhammad

ASSIGNMENTS

● It is important to understand that there were no pictures or sculptures of the Prophet made during his life-time. Many Muslims believe that there should be no pictures of the Prophet. Others only show him with his face veiled, as in the picture. In real life Muhammad did not wear a veil. Why do you think he is shown like this? Go back and reread the passages on the second spread and the passage from Rumi on page 19. Write an explanation of why you think the Prophet's face is veiled in the picture.

● Read some other Hadith stories. Take one or two which you find particularly interesting and explain why.

KEY WORDS

Hadith

SALAH: MUSLIM PRAYER

Every devout Muslim will perform the Muslim prayer, **Salah**, five times each day. Salah is one of the most important and distinctive of the five Pillars of Islam. One Muslim explained its meaning:

'The first thing to be understood is that Salah is ordained by God for Muslims. It is laid down how a Muslim should pray; the times for the prayer; and the way it is to be performed. The pattern has been given to us by Allah and we do not choose our own way of praying.'

There are two important terms used to describe the actions of the prayer: **Rakah** and **Sujdah**. Each word explains an important part of Salah.

Rakah

Rakah refers to the number of times a Muslim repeats the action of bowing during the prayer. The number of Rakahs varies between two and four depending on which of the five daily prayers is being performed. The Rakahs create a rhythm of movements based on a pattern given by the Prophet Muhammad. So as Muslims pray they are conscious of following a rhythm used by the Holy Prophet.

● Many people of different faiths use different patterns of movement when they pray. How do you think a rhythm of movement might help people pray?

Sujdah

The second important word is Sujdah. One of the key moments in the Salah is when Muslims touch their foreheads on the ground. The English word for this is 'prostration'.

● The picture shows Muslims performing Sujdah. Looked at from the outside this might appear to be a slightly odd position. Discuss how it might feel to be in this position. What do you think the meaning of Sujdah might be?

One Muslim explained its meaning:

'It is a symbol of total submission to your Creator. Having placed your forehead on the ground you have reduced yourself to the lowest level. It is a reminder that you should not be so proud that you are not willing to bend your will to Allah. It is also a very peaceful moment which reminds us that Islam means both submission and peace. You cannot have one without the other. You do not remain like this. You soon stand up again and feel the power of being human. But then you realise that your power comes from God and you should use it properly.'

ASSIGNMENTS

● Research precisely how a Muslim prays. You will need to find out the details of the movements and words used during the prayer. Produce a flow diagram to show the pattern of movement. Write a short piece to explain how you understand the movements.

● In some religions it is common to remain still while you pray or meditate. Research some examples. What reasons would you give for why it might be better to use movement and why it might be preferable to remain still?

KEY WORDS

Salah   Rakah   Sujdah

Muslims performing
Sujdah in England

A SPACE FOR PRAYER

The picture shows a Muslim praying in a Yorkshire factory where he works. Imagine what it might feel like to pray in a place like this. Notice how he has created a space for his prayer. Muslims believe it is important to create the right space in which to pray – but it is possible to pray anywhere.

There are two central points about the space in which a Muslim prays. Firstly, it

is necessary to be facing towards **Makkah** in Saudi Arabia. If a Muslim is unsure of the direction of Makkah, he or she will use a compass to work out which way to face. Secondly, it is important that the space is clean and dry. It is not necessary to pray on a mat, although they are often used to help to create a space around the Muslim. A Muslim explained:

'It is important that I do not lose concentration while I pray. If anyone walks in front of me during the prayer my mind may wander and it would break my prayer. To avoid this I create a space around myself. I might put a chair in front of me to mark out an area, or place a stick on the ground in front of me. It is remarkable how simply marking out a space helps with concentration.'

● Try going into an open area and seeing what difference it makes to your ability to concentrate if you mark out some kind of space around you. Discuss the experience with the group.

A focus for prayer

Many religious people use some kind of object in front of them to help them concentrate. You can probably think of some examples. Although a Muslim will face towards Makkah, there is nothing in front of the person praying to help them to concentrate. Why is this?

'There is no focal point when you pray. Nothing can represent God, so the concentration during Muslim prayer is on the actions and words you will be involved in. You begin the prayer by washing yourself, which is called **Wudu**. From that moment you are preparing your mind to concentrate on the act of worship. You do not focus on any object outside yourself. Your whole attention is on your relationship with Allah. Even when we are in the mosque there is no object in front of us. The focal point of the mosque is an empty niche which simply shows the direction of Makkah. Most Muslims pray with their eyes looking downwards to help their concentration.'

ASSIGNMENTS

● Look at the picture. How has the Muslim tried to create a space in which he will be able to concentrate in the middle of the factory? You may still feel this is a strange place to pray. Discuss your ideas about why it might be difficult but valuable to pray in a place like this.

● Research some information on the washing ritual (Wudu) which occurs before the prayer. Find out the ways in which this action is different from an ordinary act of washing. Imagine you are the man in the picture and write a dialogue in which you explain the washing ritual to a non-Muslim.

KEY WORDS

Makkah   Wudu

THE MOSQUE

● The picture shows the inside of the dome of a mosque in Cordoba, Spain. Study the picture carefully to work out exactly what it is you are looking at. How many of the ideas which you have understood about Islam are reflected in this picture? Discuss your ideas in a group.

A **mosque** is simply a place of prayer. As you have already discovered, Muslims can pray anywhere. So why do they have particular buildings in which to pray?

● Look back at the pictures on pages 25 and 26. Try to imagine how the experience of the people in the two pictures might be different.

Even when Muslims pray alone in their home or workplace they are aware of the whole community of Muslims praying together. All Muslims will be facing Makkah and all will be performing the same actions and saying the same words. At the close of the prayer each Muslim will turn his head to the right and the left to acknowledge the other Muslims praying at that moment – even if they cannot see anyone else! The idea of being aware of the whole world-wide community of Muslims is very important in Islam.

'Because the prayer is set down, you feel that all Muslims around you are part of a single community. If one person's prayers are answered it embraces all of us. In the prayer we say "God grant us [not just me] all the things we need for this world and the world after." So, if my prayers are answered, then it includes everyone else. If my mind wanders, but someone else has concentrated, then I am included in their prayer.'

Jum'ah prayer

The Friday midday prayer in the mosque, called **Jum'ah prayer**, is particularly important. All male Muslims in the area will try to join together for that prayer. It shows the unity of all Muslims throughout the world. It also helps each Muslim develop his own life of prayer:

'We encourage congregational rather than individual prayer because within the congregation if my mind wanders a little bit, someone else's mind will not wander and so there is an overall concentration – a supportive concentration on what we are doing. During the prayer we stand together in close lines. No one has any special place and everyone is equal at the time of prayer. We feel a physical closeness which reminds us of the importance of the whole community.'

ASSIGNMENTS

● Look again at the picture. Create a design of your own to show the idea of unity. Write a short piece to explain your design.

● Research more details about the design of a mosque. Produce a plan of a mosque and label its important features. Explain why a mosque is designed in the way it is.

● Imagine you are a Muslim who is trying to gain permission to leave work to attend Friday prayer in the mosque. Write a letter explaining why it is important for you to be present in the mosque.

KEY WORDS

mosque   Jum'ah prayer

THE TIMES OF PRAYER

'He who observes his five-times daily prayer will be protected from evil deeds and evil thoughts.' *Hadith*

A Muslim is required to pray five times every day. Each Salah has an Arabic name and should take place during a particular part of the day.

Morning	Fajr
Early afternoon	Zuhr
Late afternoon	Asr
Sunset	Maghrib
Night	Isha

The two pictures show Muslims praying in England and Saudi Arabia

● Discuss with a partner your reaction to the idea of praying five times each day. Can you think of any reasons to pray in such a routine way? Why do you think these times might have been chosen?

We asked two Muslims to tell us about the value of praying so regularly and why the morning prayer is significant:

'Each prayer reminds me of my accountability for all I am doing during the day. It is as if I settle my account with God five times a day. So by the time the end of the day comes I am thinking about everything I have done and everything I have received during that day. The prayer in the morning is important. Sleep is an imitation of death. So waking is like a time of resurrection. The first prayer of the day is a sense of being resurrected to start a new day.'

'Doing things in a routine way can be monotonous. Salah is different. Each time I pray I feel refreshed and reassured. Prayer is like giving you new blood. It gives me energy and renews me. Prayer in the morning is very refreshing – it is like a wash before going to work. It is a preparation to carry out the daily duties.'

There are other questions we might ask about this pattern of daily prayers:

How much time do you spend praying? Is it really possible to concentrate properly when you pray so often?

What happens if you miss Salah for some reason?

We asked one Muslim for his answers to these questions:

'It is important that I concentrate hard when I pray. Our span of concentration is very short so the Salah prayer is brief. The prayer usually takes about five minutes. If my mind wanders to other thoughts I forget that prayer. So, if I catch myself thinking about the shopping my wife asked me to do, then I stop the prayer and start again. If I miss a prayer it does worry me. The times for prayer are very significant and it would have to be something very important which would make me miss my prayer. I would then try to make up the prayer I missed at another time. Anyone who just forgot a prayer would not have kept to the requirements of being a Muslim.'

ASSIGNMENTS

● Look back at the two quotes about morning prayer. The two Muslims use different words to interpret their experience of the morning Fajr prayer. Explain the differences and imagine how you think they might interpret their experiences of the final night Isha prayer.

● Non-Muslims often suggest that Salah is 'just a routine'. Write a script for a radio interview on Muslim prayer in which you explain why Salah is more than 'just a routine'.

● How would you describe the mood of the figures in the picture? Explain how this mood reflects what you now understand about Islam.

THE MEANING OF SALAH

● You have now read about some of the details of Muslim prayer. Look closely at this picture of a Muslim woman at prayer. How would you summarise what you know about the reasons *why* Muslims pray? Note down at least four points and compare your ideas with others in your group.

We asked one Muslim about her feelings when she prays:

'Prayer does not diminish or increase God one iota. Everything belongs to God and we, as human beings, are trustees of everything in the world. We are accountable for all our actions. Our prayers are periods when we account for our actions. We are not trying to persuade or influence Allah in any way. In our prayers there are thanks for the period from one prayer to another. There is an asking for forgiveness for any wrong actions since we last prayed. There is a hope for ourselves, other people and the world around us.'

Accounting for your life

One important idea in this passage is that, at the time of prayer, a Muslim accounts for his or her actions since the time of the previous prayer. After any period of time a Muslim senses the need to give thanks, ask forgiveness and look for hope in the future.

● Look back over the last day and try to identify some of your own experiences under these three headings: Thanks, Forgiveness, Hope. What value do you think there might be in looking back and forward in this way?

Another important idea in the passage quoted above is that Muslim prayer is not an attempt to persuade or influence God. One popular misunderstanding of prayer is that it is a way of trying to get God to change His mind about something. Muslims suggest that they do not pray in order to influence God but in order to change themselves. God does not need our prayers, but we do!

There is a Muslim tradition that one day the Prophet Muhammad was asked by one of his followers, 'Who is the worst thief?' The Prophet's reply was perhaps a little surprising. He answered that the worst thief is 'The one who cheats in his prayer'.

ASSIGNMENTS

● People have different ideas about the purpose and value of prayer. It was suggested above that prayer is not about trying to change God but to change ourselves. Discuss these ideas and write a piece to summarise your own thoughts about this.

● Imagine you have the opportunity to meet the woman in the picture. Prepare a series of questions you would want to ask her about Muslim prayer. Take one or two of the questions and imagine how you think she might reply. You may wish to discuss this in pairs before writing your own answer.

CELEBRATIONS

RAMADAN

> The Muslim fasts because, as a believer in God, he wishes to carry out God's commands and he understands that God wishes him to fast from dawn to sunset during the month of Ramadan. But why should God want him to undertake this every year or at all? God, who does nothing without purpose, is surely not interested in imposing upon His creatures a meaningless ritual. He asks human beings to do things for their own benefit.
>
> (*Islam From Within*)

The fourth of the five Pillars of Islam is the requirement on Muslims to fast during the month of **Ramadan**. The name for the fast is **Saum**. The fast means that Muslims will not eat and drink during the hours of daylight.

● The passage quoted above suggests that the fast is not a meaningless activity. What reasons do you think might be given for the value of fasting?

As the fast is meant for the benefit of those who follow it, it is not a requirement for all Muslims. The list below shows the five groups of Muslims who are not required to fast, although anyone in the first three groups ought to try to make up the days they missed at a later time:

Anyone who is sick or might become ill if they fasted

Anyone who is travelling long distances and finds it impossible to fast properly
Any woman who is pregnant or has just given birth
Anyone who is too old to fast without suffering
Young children

It is common for Muslim children to fast for one or two days so that they feel part of the celebration and begin to learn self-discipline.

Why fast?

Muslims believe that the month of daytime fasting is very valuable. It is the time in the year when they concentrate on their relationship with Allah and develop self-discipline. Fasting has various benefits:

It reminds Muslims of the needs of the poor.
It develops self-control.
It helps to clean out your body and makes you physically healthier.
It slows you down and reduces stress.
It encourages you to recognise what is really essential in life.

Ramadan is a time when Muslims will try to be more devout in their prayers. They will often try to read through the Qur'an during this month and spend more time reflecting on their religious life.

ASSIGNMENTS

● The picture shows a Muslim family sitting down to break their fast after sunset during the month of Ramadan. The meal is called **Iftar**, which means 'breaking the fast'. Work in a group to produce a short dialogue between the mother and her children as she answers their questions about why it is valuable to fast.

● Try to follow the fast for one day. Write an account of your reactions and feelings. How did your body respond? Did it help you to understand some of the ideas in this spread?

KEY WORDS

Ramadan   Saum   Iftar

A family eating an Iftar meal in Bahrain

CELEBRATION AND SHARING

Eid-ul-Fitr is one of the two most important Muslim festivals and it occurs on the day after the end of the Ramadan fast. Because the Muslim calendar is lunar, the celebration begins when the new moon is sighted to show that the old month, Ramadan, is over. It is never entirely certain when the new moon will appear so there is always an element of excitement in Muslim homes at this time. Will the new moon appear tonight or not? Will we celebrate tomorrow or the day after?

The festival involves feasting, exchanging gifts and, generally, enjoying the experience of celebration.

One of the purposes of fasting is to enable Muslims to understand the experience of being hungry, and so appreciate what it might be like to starve. It is not just a matter of thinking and feeling, but also of taking action. On the festival of Eid-ul-Fitr Muslims make an offering of a sum of money which is given to the needy. The money is often sent to a Muslim Welfare organisation to be distributed to those who are suffering in some way.

Zakah

The third Pillar of Islam is known as **Zakah** and it involves each adult Muslim making a payment of approximately 2$\frac{1}{2}$ per cent of their wealth to those in need each year.

Zakah has two meanings. The basic meaning is 'legal almsgiving', in other words, a requirement to help redistribute wealth within the Muslim community. It is now usually a matter of individual conscience whether the money is paid, but in traditional Muslim societies it was common for the money to be collected by the government as a form of tax.

The second meaning of Zakah is 'purity'. It is quite acceptable in Muslim societies to be wealthy. However, it is understood that wealth brings with it responsibilities. The payment of Zakah is part of these responsibilities and it shows that you realise that your wealth has to be used properly. It purifies the rest of your wealth. It is a reminder to those with wealth that everything comes from, and returns to, God.

The picture shows another form of 'giving' in the Muslim community. Money is being collected at Friday prayer in the mosque in Coventry. It is used to support the work of the mosque.

Zakah and Salah, the Muslim prayer, are often described as the two basic religious activities for Muslims. While Salah is about the individual's relationship with God, Zakah is about their relationship with the rest of humanity.

Salah helps to create peace and harmony within the individual. Zakah is a way of helping the Muslim community as a whole to create this peace and harmony.

ASSIGNMENTS

- Imagine you are one of the Muslims in the picture. You are asked to explain the value of your action. What answer would you give?

- Research more details about the celebrations of Eid-ul-Fitr. Write a diary account of the day, imagining you were present during the celebration.

- It is very common in religion for celebrations to include giving a donation to charity. Think of some examples and explain why you think a celebration is a good time to make such donations.

KEY WORDS

Eid-ul-Fitr   Zakah

Zakah being collected
at a mosque in Coventry

BIRTH

● Imagine you have just become a parent. To celebrate the birth, you decide to write down the most important piece of advice which you would like to pass on to your child when he or she is older. What would it be?

The day of the birth

When a Muslim family has a child it is seen as a gift from Allah. The parents hold a simple ceremony to show their feelings about the event. The ceremony involves whispering the call to prayer (the **Adhan**) into the baby's ear. It is important to parents that this is the first thing their child hears – even though the baby will not understand at the time. In Britain this celebration often happens in the maternity unit of the hospital.

The seventh day

Seven days after the baby is born, a second ceremony is often performed. On this day it is usual to announce the name of the baby to a gathering of friends and relations. Read what two Muslims told us about the names they chose for their children:

'It is traditional in our family for children to take the name of one of their grandparents or great-grandparents. It is important to us to keep these family bonds. My grandfather was called Ali, after the name of the Prophet Muhammad's son-in-law, so that was the name we chose for our son. The names of the Prophet's family and close companions are often chosen.'

'We named our son Salim, which means "peace". This is one of the Beautiful Names of God and we hoped that choosing this name would bring blessings from God to our son.'

Aqeeqa

On this seventh day it is also common to perform **Aqeeqa**. The baby's head is carefully shaved and the hair is weighed. The family then celebrate the birth by giving the same weight of either gold or silver to those in need in the community. The new baby has made its first act of charity towards others.

A family often asks a local Muslim butcher to slaughter either two animals (if it is a boy) or one animal (if it is a girl). Some of the meat is eaten by the family and friends at the celebration. The rest is given to those who are in need in the community.

ASSIGNMENTS

● Look at the picture. Imagine you are the parent of the new child. Write down your feelings and thoughts about this day as a record to give the child when he or she grows up. Include a short explanation of what happened on the first and seventh days and explain why you felt it was important to do the things you did.

● Find out the words of the Adhan, the call to prayer. Why do you think these words are chosen as the first thing a baby will hear?

KEY WORDS

Adhan   Aqeeqa

The Adhan is whispered into a new-born baby's ear

MUSLIM MARRIAGE

Islamic marriage reflects many of the important aspects of the Muslim faith. Many Muslims believe that a marriage is likely to be successful if it follows traditional Islamic practice. This includes having an arranged marriage.

The arranged marriage

Look at the couple in the picture. They are no doubt a little nervous about this moment. The moment of marriage is

highly charged with some very different feelings: excitement, joy, nervousness. In particular you may find couples wondering just for a moment: Have I made the right decision?

● What is the best basis for choosing a marriage partner? How would you rank the following in order of their importance?
Similar background   Being in love   Similar interests   Mutual respect   Similar education   Similar attitudes to life   Family freindship   Equal social status.
Discuss your rank order with others.

For many Muslims, 'being in love' is seen as a poor basis for getting married. It is common to hear Muslims say that the difference between Muslim and Western marriage is that 'In the West you marry the person you love; in Muslim marriage we love the person we marry.' For many Muslims it is understood that marriage is a matter of two families coming together. The families arrange the marriage for their children by deciding which partner is likely to make a stable happy marriage. It is not uncommon to hear Muslims express their feelings like this:

'Marriage in the West seems unsuccessful. One in three marriages break up. Muslim marriages are usually successful. Divorce is uncommon. A marriage in Islam is between two families, not just two individuals. This means there is support from the families and the marriage is stronger.'

An arranged marriage does not mean the individuals have no choice in the matter. Once a family decide on someone whom they think would make a good marriage partner the couple are introduced to one another. It is quite acceptable for them to refuse to marry if they feel that it would not work. Alternatively, if a Muslim man finds a woman whom he believes would make a good marriage partner, he is likely to take her to meet his parents.

'My parents have a lot more wisdom than me. If they feel the partnership would not work they will say no and I will respect their decision. They will give me their reasons and I am confident that they will be right. Involving the two families in the decision about marriage is the right way to achieve a successful, happy marriage.'

ASSIGNMENTS

● Design and carry out a simple survey to find out about people's views on arranged marriage. Imagine you are a Muslim who wants to explain to a non-Muslim friend why you have agreed to have an arranged marriage. Write a letter to your friend explaining your reasons.

● Research some further information about Muslim marriage. Make a list of any other details you can discover.

A Muslim wedding in Pakistan

THE RITUALS OF DEATH

Dealing with death

Every religious tradition has to face the fact of death. Islam has a series of rituals to deal with the fact of the dead body. In many ways these rituals tell us much about how Muslims understand death.

'As a Muslim approaches death, we would try to turn their face towards Makkah and recite the first of the Pillars of our faith: "There is no God but Allah." It is important that the dying person should be given this final

reminder of the most basic of our beliefs. We believe that once the soul has passed from the grave it will be questioned by two angels about its life. As soon as the person dies we clean the body and straighten the limbs. The body will be given a bath and, hopefully, the burial will occur within a few hours of the death. We say a number of prayers for the deceased and finally bury the body facing towards Makkah. As you would expect, sections of the Qur'an are read at the funeral and for some days a period of mourning continues.'

Death as a return

For Muslims, death is a return. The soul of the departed is being returned to God. At death the soul leaves the body and passes through the doorway to the next stage of existence. One of the more common prayers used at the funeral explains many of the Muslim beliefs about the afterlife of the soul:

> Allah, do forgive her and have mercy upon her and make her secure and overlook her shortcomings, and give her an honoured place in Paradise. Make her

A Muslim funeral in England

place of entry spacious, and wash her clean with water and snow and ice and cleanse her of all wrong as Thou dost clean a piece of white cloth of dirt. Give her a home better than her home and a family better than her family and a spouse better than her spouse, and admit her into Paradise, and shield her from the torment of the grave and the torment of the fire.

Muslims believe that after death there is a period of trial in which the person's life will be judged.

> The Day of Judgement is nothing but a trial to show each person why he is being sent to heaven or hell, because of his deeds. It's not because God has decided that you should be sent to heaven or hell, it's because your past deeds exist and will be shown and explained to you.
>
> (J. Bowker, *Worlds of Faith*, BBC)

ASSIGNMENTS

- Prepare some simple guidelines for a local hospital to help them understand what must be done in the case of the death of a Muslim and why each detail is important.
- How do Muslim beliefs about life after death compare with your own? Write a dialogue between yourself and a Muslim in which both ideas are explained.

PILGRIMAGE

THE KA'BA

For Muslims, their lifetime experience is to go on the **Hajj** – the pilgrimage to the Holy City of Makkah. Hajj is the fifth of the five Pillars of Islam. It is an obligation that once during their lifetime Muslims should perform the pilgrimage, as long as they can afford to do so.

The pilgrimage takes place during the first days of the lunar month of Dhu'l-Hijjah. It is not uncommon for as many as two million pilgrims to visit Makkah at that time. It is the climax of the pattern of worship in a Muslim's life.

The Ka'ba

One of the most important moments of Hajj is the visit to the **Ka'ba** in Makkah. According to Muslim tradition, the Ka'ba was the first house of worship to Allah and was built by the Prophet Abraham (Ibrahim). Muslims believe that before Ibrahim the places of worship were built by polytheists – those who worshipped many gods. Ibrahim's building contained no objects – this showed that God lies beyond everything that is created and that nothing can represent God.

According to tradition, the Makkans soon fell away from this belief and returned to polytheism, placing many idols inside the Ka'ba. The Prophet Muhammad finally restored the Ka'ba to its true state by removing all the idols and returning the building to the purpose for which it was built by Ibrahim. One Muslim wrote of his experience of visiting the Ka'ba:

Pilgrims seemed to be on top of each other, there were so many, lying, sitting, sleeping, praying, walking.... Then I saw the Ka'ba, a huge black stone house in the middle of the Great Mosque. It was being circumambulated by thousands upon thousands of praying pilgrims, both sexes, and every size, shape, colour, and race in the world.... Upon entering the Mosque, the pilgrim should try to kiss the Ka'ba if possible, but if the crowds prevent him getting that close, he touches it and if the crowds prevent that, he raises his hand and cries out 'Allahu akbar' (God is Great). I could not get within yards. My feeling there in the House of God was one of numbness.

(*Islam From Within*)

ASSIGNMENTS

● The picture shows the pilgrims circling the Ka'ba. One writer has described this as a 'human whirlpool'. Imagine yourself in this crowd and write a piece of poetry or prose to express what your feelings might be.

● Research any further information you can find about the Ka'ba. Use this information to explain why the writer in the quote seems to feel such a sense of excitement about seeing it for the first time.

KEY WORDS

Hajj   Ka'ba

HAJJ: MUHAMMAD AND ARAFAT

The picture shows the pilgrims near the **Mount of Mercy** on the **Plain of Arafat** just outside Makkah.

It is the second day of the pilgrimage and pilgrims will remain at Arafat for the rest of the day. They will pray, read from the Qur'an, meet with other Muslims from throughout the world, and listen to sermons from leading Muslims.

The **haji** (the name adopted by any male who has performed the Hajj; women are known as **hajin**) will have a sense of God at the centre of their thoughts. However, this is also a place where the memory of the Prophet Muhammad will be very strong.

The last sermon

The Mount of Mercy was the place where the Prophet delivered his final sermon, which sums up the heart of his message. He died 81 days after delivering the sermon. The following is an extract:

'My people, listen carefully to my words. I do not know if I will meet you again like this. My people, just as you keep this month of the pilgrimage and this day and this city sacred, so you should keep the life and property of every Muslim sacred. Reflect on my words. I leave behind two things, the Qur'an and the example of my life. If you follow these, you will not fail. No prophet or messenger will follow me. All who listen to me pass on my words to others. May the last ones understand my words better than those of you who hear me now.'

● The sermon summarises the basic ideas of Islam. From this extract, which ideas can you identify? How would you explain the last sentence?

Not all Muslims react to the pilgrimage in the same way. One haji recorded his experience of being at Arafat in a diary:

From our camp, I can see the Mount of Mercy, a small hill from which the Prophet gave his last sermon. Between 90,000 and 100,000 people accompanied him on the Farewell Pilgrimage. I am told that there will be a series of speakers and preachers there today, but I do not want to join the crowd listening to them. To truly understand my brothers, with whom I want to enter into communion, I feel I must experience some quiet reading and meditation. It is only by fully understanding myself that I shall be able to understand others. As if to strengthen me in my urge for meditation, silence seems to be spreading throughout the tens of thousands of people whom I had found too noisy for my liking a short while ago.

(*Mecca – The Muslim Pilgrimage*, Paddington Press)

ASSIGNMENTS

● The picture gives some idea of what it is like to be on the Mount of Mercy. Read the diary extract again and imagine the writer being approached by a fellow Muslim who tries to encourage him to listen to some of the preachers. Write a dialogue between them as the diary writer tries to explain his feelings.

● An experience like the Hajj is not simply a matter of making a visit. Muslims hope it will change them and help them develop their faith. From what you have read so far, how do you think the Hajj might change a person who is involved? Write a piece explaining your ideas.

KEY WORDS

Mount of Mercy   Plain of Arafat
haji   hajin

THE FESTIVAL OF SACRIFICE

The festival of **Eid-ul-Adha** is the second main festival in the Muslim calendar. For Muslims on the Hajj it occurs during their three-day stay at the small village of Mina, after they have left the Plain of Arafat. The festival is also celebrated by Muslims all over the world and it is an opportunity to feel they are part of the pilgrimage, even though they have remained at home.

The 'Stoning of Satan' at Mina

The central part of the festival is the sacrifice of an animal (usually a sheep or goat) by each pilgrim. Part of the meat is eaten by the pilgrim, or by the Muslim family if it is being celebrated at home. The rest of the meat is traditionally given to the poor. The festival reminds Muslims that they should be ready to give up their worldly possessions and share with those less fortunate than themselves.

In the modern world the amount sacrificed is often much more than is needed by those who are starving in the local area. One Muslim expressed his concern about this act of sacrifice:

In an age of food shortages in many parts of the world, people question this slaughtering of animals. Most of the carcasses have to be destroyed as rapidly as possible to avoid stench and disease. It is a problem that has concerned not only the Saudi Arabian government but also the religious authorities and other Muslim countries for several decades now.

(*Mecca – The Muslim Pilgrimage*)

● Discuss this quote. Why do you think this has become a problem in the modern world where Muslims often live in communities which are less close-knit?

Ibrahim's sacrifice

The sacrifice is a reminder of a story from the Qur'an about the Prophet Ibrahim:

The Prophet Ibrahim dreamt that God commanded him to take his son Ishmael to a place called Mina where he was to sacrifice his son to show his obedience. The following day, Ibrahim took his son to Mina. On the way, Satan came to Ibrahim three times – tempting him to disobey God. Ibrahim ignored Satan and when he reached the place of sacrifice he raised his knife, closed his eyes and plunged the blade into his son's body. When he opened his eyes he discovered that God had replaced Ishmael with a ram and that the boy was standing safely by him.

The story shows the depth of Ibrahim's faith. The festival is a way of reminding Muslims that their faith goes back to the Prophet Ibrahim. It helps Muslims realise how strong the faith of the Prophet was – a model for all Muslims.

ASSIGNMENTS

● Imagine you have been asked to chair a discussion about the practice of sacrifice at the festival. Work with a partner to plan the issues and questions you want to use to guide your discussion.

● The temptation of Ibrahim by Satan, mentioned in the story above, also plays a part in the Hajj rituals. The picture shows part of these rituals. Find out the details and write a piece to explain their meaning.

KEY WORDS

Eid-ul-Adha

THE MEANING OF HAJJ

A complex celebration like the pilgrimage to Makkah has many meanings. Each pilgrim will bring away their own personal experience.

● From what you have read about the pilgrimage, what different meanings have you noticed? The following words may provide some ideas:
Unity, Equality, Sacrifice, Peace, Remembering.

One central meaning of the Hajj is that it is a drawing-together of the whole of a Muslim's life and belief.

Drawing together

As the Muslim spends time at Makkah, he or she will know that all of space and time are focused on this place. For a Muslim, the Ka'ba in Makkah is the centre of the world. It is the place towards which Muslims turn when they pray. Before coming to Makkah, the Muslim faced towards the stone house of God from afar. Now Muslims are able to circle around, touch and perhaps even kiss the place which has been a focus of so much of their lives.

It is also the place which gathers together the whole of human history. By tradition, the small black stone which is placed in one of the outside corners of the Ka'ba was a stone which fell from heaven when Adam, the first human being, came to earth. Ibrahim built the Ka'ba, and, finally, the Prophet Muhammad was born in Makkah and came to understand that the Ka'ba was the first house of God.

A gathering of unity

The Hajj is also an expression of the unity of all Muslims throughout the world. At any Hajj there will be representatives from every country in which Muslims live. Looking back at the pictures on the last few pages you will notice that the dress of the pilgrims does not reflect the wide number of different countries from which pilgrims come. It is a requirement that all men on Hajj wear two simple pieces of white cloth, called **Ihram**. Women also dress simply while at Makkah. Ihram means 'devoting yourself to God' and it emphasises that, while on Hajj, a pilgrim's mind should be focused on God alone. The clothing also stresses the unity of all Muslims.

This great gathering has another meaning for many Muslims. It is a reminder of the Great Day of Judgement to come. On that day all Muslims will be gathered and any differences between them which may have seemed important on earth will count for nothing. On that day the only important difference between Muslims will be the differences in the quality of their faith and religious life.

One writer described the Hajj as 'a journey to a common hearth-fire from which the pilgrim could carry back the renewed and restored flame of faith to their own community'.

The diary writer quoted on previous pages ended his Hajj with these words:

> My own feelings on leaving Makkah were that I was not returning, but merely setting out.
>
> (*Mecca – The Muslim Pilgrimage*)

Young pilgrims in Ihram dress

ASSIGNMENTS

● Look back over the pictures on the last four spreads on Hajj. Which of the pictures do you find most powerful and best sums up what seems to be important about the meaning of Hajj? Imagine you are explaining your choice of picture to someone who has no knowledge of Islam. What explanation would you give?

● Reread the final quotes. From what you have read, what meaning can you give to these words? Imagine you are writing a letter home at the end of the Hajj to explain why you feel you are 'merely setting out' instead of 'returning'.

KEY WORDS

Ihram

THE MUSLIM COMMUNITY

The Islamic calendar began with an event which Muslims believe was a new starting-point in the whole history of humanity. You might assume it would be the birth or death of the Prophet Muhammad or perhaps the date when the Qur'an first began to be revealed to Muhammad. Both answers would be wrong.

The Muslim calendar is dated from the day when the first true Muslim community was formed. The community, called the **Umma,** was founded on the day Muhammad and his followers migrated from the city of Makkah to the town of

Muslims after Friday prayers in Coventry

Madinah. This day, which falls in 622 of the Christian calendar, was the beginning of year 1 of the Muslim era. The Arabic word for the migration is **Hijrah**.

The Hijrah

Muhammad saw the need to find a place where a new community could be formed which based its life on the Qur'an. He decided to migrate to Madinah. The Hijrah was a difficult and dangerous journey. Muslim tradition tells that Muhammad's own life was threatened during the migration. The decision to date the calendar from the Hijrah shows how important the formation of the Umma is to Muslims.

Islam as a complete way of life

Many Muslims believe that the whole of life should follow the guidance of the Qur'an. This means that ideally a Muslim needs to live in a community in which every aspect of life is shaped by Islamic ideas. The Umma is that community. Muslims believe this is the only way in which real peace and harmony in a community can be achieved.

Many Muslims feel a strong sense of community. One Muslim, living in Britain, explained how his daily pattern of prayer helps create a sense of the unity of the Umma:

'The prayer has never changed and never will because it is from God. The most important thing about Salah is that it is a bond for all Muslims. I know that all Muslims will be praying in the same way as me, all facing to Makkah, all saying the same words and performing the same actions. If I go to China I may not find it easy to communicate with the people but I know that at the time of prayer we will all be standing in the same manner, saying the same Arabic words. This is a real community bond. As I say my prayers in Britain I am aware that there is a great circle of Muslims throughout the world joining with me. We form an invisible series of concentric circles all round the globe.'

ASSIGNMENTS

● Look again at the explanation about prayer. Select another Muslim activity which you think might create a feeling of the Umma, the bond of the Muslim community. Imagine you are a Muslim and write a short passage showing how the activity creates this bond.

● Muslims believe that peace and harmony are achieved in a community only if all members share a common set of values. Some people believe we have lost this sense of community in Britain today. What is your group's opinion of this? Write one or two paragraphs explaining your various points of view.

KEY WORDS

Umma   Hijrah

A CODE FOR LIFE

● The picture shows a plan of a Muslim town. Can you
identify the mosque on the plan? What do you notice about
the design of the town? Does this relate to any of the ideas
about Islam which you have now understood?

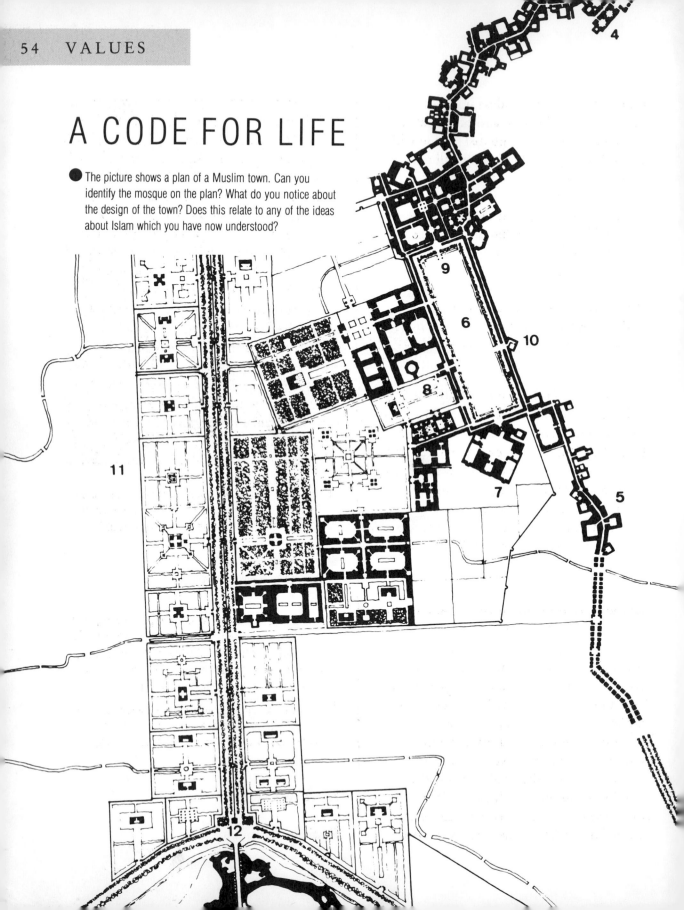

One of the important ideas in Islam is that the life of each Muslim and of the Islamic community should be guided by the will of God. As human beings we will only achieve real peace and harmony if we follow a pattern of life. Everything needs to be shaped by a pattern based on the will of Allah. This includes education, business, health, politics, town planning and architecture.

● Look back at the spread on Shirk. Remind yourself why Muslims believe that suffering is caused by placing something else at the centre of life instead of, or as well as, God.

The Qur'an and the traditions about the Prophet Muhammad are used by Muslims to work out how they should live their lives. The Qur'an, however, does not give direct answers on every point. It has been necessary for the Umma, the Muslim community, to develop a framework of laws and rules based on the Qur'an. This framework is called the **Shari'ah**.

Shari'ah

'Shari'ah' is based on the Arabic word for 'road'. It is seen as a road that leads from God and to God. It covers all aspects of human life, not just religious duties. In an ideal Muslim community everything would be based on Muslim principles.

The reality for many Muslims is that they live in countries where the Shari'ah is not at the centre of the community's life. A Muslim teacher in the UK, explained:

'Life in Britain is not guided by the Shari'ah, our Muslim law. Many of the ways of life in Britain are not in agreement with the Shari'ah. For example, in schools the timetable is not organised to allow Muslim pupils and teachers to pray at the normal times for Salah. Sometimes this creates a problem for us and we have to decide how to cope. So, as a teacher, I often find I cannot pray at the correct time because I am teaching. It would be wrong for me to stop my lessons and disrupt the pupils' education, so I just quietly remind myself that it is the time for prayer without anyone knowing it. I would then say the prayer I have missed a little later.'

● Discuss what you think about the last point. From what you know of Islam, can you think of any other reasons why it might be difficult to be a Muslim and live in the UK?

ASSIGNMENTS

● In what ways do you think town planning and the design of architecture might affect the quality of people's lives? How might they affect our sense of peace and harmony? Design your own town plan based on the idea of making a place which would create harmony in people's lives.

● Discuss the last quote about prayer. Write a short article for the local press explaining some other difficulties which Muslims face when they live in a non-Muslim society.

KEY WORDS

Shari'ah

HALAL AND KHALIFAH

The way of life laid out in the Shari'ah, the Muslim law, is not just a list of things Muslims cannot do. It also includes things they are required to do, recommended to do and permitted to do.

One word which is part of the Islamic way of life may be familiar to you: **halal**.

Many Muslims believe that non-Muslims have seriously misunderstood Islam. One example is the way in which this word is often misinterpreted. Halal is often associated with halal meat, and non-Muslims have pictures of cruel slaughter and a lack of care for animals. We need to

know the meaning of the word. Halal is simply the Arabic word for 'permitted'.

We asked a Muslim to explain how he understood this:

'As a Muslim I believe that there are guidelines about what I should and should not eat. We are allowed to eat meat – although pork is not permitted. We believe, however, that all animals are part of God's creation and that we should not take any life carelessly. So we have careful rules about how to slaughter animals. In particular, it is important to pronounce the name of Allah over any animal that is killed. By saying this we believe that no animal will be killed thoughtlessly. By repeating the name of God you are always reminded that the animal is a creature of God. If the meat has been correctly slaughtered according to Muslim law it is called halal and we are permitted to eat it.'

Khalifah

A central Muslim belief is that, as humans, we have a particular responsibility for the rest of the natural world. We are **khalifah**, meaning God's representatives on earth. The natural world will follow the Will of

A Halal butcher in Birmingham

God unless it is damaged by the actions of human beings. One Muslim explained how he understands this:

'At the moment in prayer when my forehead touches the ground I am reminded that I am responsible for all animal and plant life – even the most insignificant insect in the world. We are all responsible for the ecology of the planet. This does not mean I have a romantic view of nature. I know that it is part of the created order of nature for animals to kill and eat each other. This keeps the ecology of the planet in balance. My goal is to understand the pattern of nature and flow with it – not to conquer it.'

ASSIGNMENTS

● There is a great deal of debate about whether the Muslim method of slaughter should be allowed. Find out more information about this debate. Imagine you are a Muslim butcher and decide to put up a notice in your shop explaining your point of view. Write the notice.

● The final quote suggests the Muslim approach to nature is to 'flow with it' rather than 'conquer it'. What do you think the difference is? What kinds of activity would mean you were 'flowing with' or 'conquering' nature? Produce two columns of ideas to show your understanding of the difference between 'flowing with' and 'conquering'.

KEY WORDS

halal   khalifah

WOMEN IN ISLAM

● Look at the two pictures. The women in both pictures are wearing traditional styles of Muslim dress. Do you find you react differently to the two pictures? Discuss as a group.

Muslims feel there is a great deal of prejudice in Britain about the situation of women in Islam. While it may be true that some Muslim women feel trapped by their faith, many accept traditional patterns of life because they sense that these are right.

Women's dress

The traditional Muslim view is that:

> Islam does not allow that a man should cast eyes upon women except his own wife in full gaze. Outside her home, she is required to wear a covering-type of dress which will make it clear to anyone who sees her that she is a modest woman who respects her own body.

Women interpret this view in different ways. While some choose to wear a 'burka' which hides their entire body, most dress in a headscarf, shalwar (baggy pants) and khameez (smock). Two women spoke about their experience, the first about her

experience of having to wear non-Muslim dress at school:

> 'I'll never forget my schooldays in Huddersfield. I was forced to tramp from one school to another in a gymslip, showing my legs, feeling naked, forced to play hockey, petrified that some member of my family might see me.'

'Wearing traditional Muslim dress is something I choose to do. I feel greater freedom this way. It means I can move around without feeling that I am being harassed or judged by my appearance. I don't have to compete with all the pictures of attractive women that dominate our society.'

Many Muslim parents would prefer to have separate-sex schools for their children and a number of private schools have been set up for this purpose. One of the pictures shows a science class in an all-girls Muslim school in England. These are not women trapped in traditional domestic roles. Their career ambitions might well include accountancy, teaching or motor mechanics.

ASSIGNMENTS

● Many non-Muslims are quick to make judgements about the experience of Muslim women. Working with one or two others in your group, select two or three pictures of Muslim women in different styles of traditional dress and carry out a survey to find out how others react to the pictures. Write a group report on your findings.

● Collect together some images of women from popular magazines and newspapers. Write a commentary on the pictures explaining how you think Muslim women might react to the images.

SUFISM

Being a Muslim means following the Shari'ah as the road which leads to peace and harmony in society. Some Muslims, however, choose to go further. They seek to move along another path which they believe will lead them to a deeper understanding of themselves and of God. These people are called **Sufis** and they follow the spiritual path of **Tariqah**.

The Mevlevi or Whirling Dervishes from Turkey

'The Shari'ah is like the circumference of a circle. It includes all of life and the goal of a Muslim is to bring all their life inside the circumference. The Tariqah, or spiritual path, is like the radius of the circle which you follow in order to come close to the centre, the heart of all truth, which is called **Haqiqah**, the Truth. Following the Shari'ah is like learning to walk properly on a flat plain. Following the Tariqah is like beginning to climb a mountain towards the peak which is Haqiqah, the Truth.'

Sufis, who follow this path of Tariqah, use a variety of different kinds of activities in order to create a deeper sense of knowing God.

Dhikr

One of the most important ideas in Sufism is **Dhikr**, which means remembrance. The rituals of Dhikr vary in different Sufi groups. Often they involve the constant repetition of the names of God. It may involve Sufis leaving their normal state of consciousness. They will lose all sense of the cares and worries of life and will concentrate their whole mind on God. Sufis describe this as the experience of **Fana**, which means a sense of losing whatever belongs to yourself and coming to know God alone. One writer describes watching a Sufi practising his ritual:

'The cadence of the singing, the dances and rituals seemed to go on vibrating in him perpetually: his head would sometimes rock rhythmically to and fro while his soul was plunged in the unfathomable mysteries of the Divine Name hidden in the Dhikr, the Remembrance. . . . He gave out an impression of unreality, so remote was he.'

One way of describing what the Sufi is seeking is to use the idea of a veil. In ordinary life we live with a veil between us and the truth. We do not see things as they really are; things are shrouded by the veil. During the spiritual practices of the path of Tariqah the veil is lifted from our mind and we see things as they really are.

ASSIGNMENTS

● The practices of the Sufis have similarities with and differences from many of the other Muslim activities described in this book. Which of the details seem to echo other Muslim practices you have discovered? How does Sufi practice seem different from other forms of Islam?

● Write a piece of poetry or prose to express what it might feel like to take part in a Sufi ritual.

● The picture shows one group of Sufis called the Mevlevi or Whirling Dervishes. Find out more about the group and write a commentary on the meaning of their sacred dance.

KEY WORDS

Sufi   Tariqah   Haqiqah   Dhikr
Fana

Glossary

Adhan Call to prayer made five times a day

Allah Arabic name for God

Aqeeqa Celebration on the seventh day after the birth of a child

Dhikr Act of remembering God

Eid-ul-Adha Festival of Sacrifice

Eid-ul-Fitr Festival to mark the end of Ramadan

Fana Sufi word for the deepest religious experience

Hadith Collection of sayings and stories of the Prophet Muhammad

hafiz Someone who has learnt the Qur'an by heart

haji Male Muslim who has completed Hajj

hajin Female Muslim who has completed Hajj

Hajj Annual pilgrimage to Makkah – the fifth Pillar of Islam

halal Anything which is permitted in Muslim law

Haqiqah Arabic word for 'truth'

Hijrah Migration of the Prophet from Makkah to Madinah

Iftar Meal which breaks the fast each evening during Ramadan

Ihram White garments worn by pilgrims on the Hajj

Islam Peace or submission to Allah

Jum'ah prayer Friday midday prayer

Ka'ba Sacred cube-shaped building in Makkah; the focus for prayer

khalifah Arabic word for humanity's responsibility for creation

Makkah The most sacred city in the Islamic world

mosque Muslim place of worship

Mount of Mercy Mountain near Makkah where Muhammad delivered his Last Sermon

Pillars of Islam The five basic requirements for being a Muslim

Plain of Arafat One of the main sites of the Muslim pilgrimage

Qur'an Sacred book of Islam

Rakah Cycle of movements and words used at prayer

Ramadan Month of the fast

Salah The five daily prayers – the second Pillar of Islam

Saum Month's fast during Ramadan – the fourth Pillar of Islam

Shahadah The Declaration of Faith – the first Pillar of Islam

Shari'ah Islamic Law

Shirk Basic sin of giving any partner to Allah

Sufi Muslim mystic

Sujdah Act of prostration during prayer

surah Chapter of the Qur'an

Tariqah Mystical Path of Islam

Tawhid Belief in the unity of Allah

Umma The Islamic community

Wudu Ritual cleansing before prayer

Zakah Almsgiving – the third Pillar of Islam

Index

Further reading

Brine, A. *Worship: An Exploration*, Macmillan, 1987

Brown, A., J. Rankin and A. Wood. *Religions*, Longman, 1988

Cragg, K. and M. Speight, *Islam From Within*, Wadsworth, 1980

Tames, R. *Islam*, Batsford, 1985
The Muslim World in *Religions of the World* series, Macdonald, 1982

Wood, A. *Being a Muslim*, Batsford, 1987

Acknowledgements

We have been unable to trace the copyright holder in the poem on page 12 from *Islamic Rhymes for Muslim Children* (pub. I.S.E.S. Educational Press, 1980) and would appreciate any information that would enable us to do so.

We are grateful to the following for permission to reproduce photographs:

Abbas/Magnum, pages **26, 30** *right*, **42, 58**; Camerapix, pages **4, 48**; Douglas Dickins, page **28**; Chris Fairclough, pages **9, 56**; Sonia Halliday Photographs, pages **23, 60**; Hutchison Library, pages **18** (photo: Dave Brinicombe), **59**; Christine Osborne, pages **33, 35, 40**; David Richardson, pages **37, 52**; Screen Ventures, London, pages **6** (photo: Peter Sanders), **13** (photo: Christopher Mould), **15** (photo: Peter Sanders), **17** (photo: Peter Sanders), **30** *left* (photo: Peter Sanders), **39** (photo: Peter Sanders), **44** (photo: Ovidio Salazar), **46** (photo: Christopher Mould), **51** (photo: Peter Sanders); Select, page **25** (photo: Richard Olivier); Frank Spooner Pictures, page **10** (photo: Son Vichith/Gamma); Israel Talby, page **20**

Cover: Girls looking at Eid cards.
Photo: Peter Sanders.

LONGMAN GROUP UK LIMITED
Longman House, Burnt Mill, Harlow,
Essex CM20 2JE, England
and Associated Companies throughout the world.

First published 1991

ISBN 0 582 02967 8

Set in 11/14 pt Garamond
Produced by Longman Group (FE) Ltd
Printed in Hong Kong

Picture research by Andrea Stern